WHEN I GROW UP

I'LL BE A MUSICIAN

BY CONNIE COLWELL MILLER

ILLUSTRATED BY SILVIA BA

AMICUS ILLUSTRATED • RIVERSTREAM

AMICUS ILLUSTRATED is published by Amicus
P.O. Box **227**, Mankato, MN 56002
www.amicuspublishing.us

Paperback edition printed by RiverStream Publishing in arrangement with Amicus.
ISBN 978-1-62243-363-6 (paperback)

LIBRARY OF CONGRESS CATALOGING-IN-PUBLICATION DATA
Miller, Connie Colwell, 1976- author.
I'll be a musician / by Connie Colwell Miller ; illustrated by Silvia Baroncelli.
pages cm. — (When I grow up—)
Summary: "A young girl practices her violin lesson and pretends to be a famous concert violinist, showing what it's like to be a professional musician"— Provided by publisher.
ISBN 978-1-60753-762-5 (library binding) — ISBN 978-1-60753-861-5 (ebook)
1. Music—Vocational guidance—Juvenile literature. I. Baroncelli, Silvia, illustration. II. Title.
ML3795.M523 2017
780.23—dc23 2015029349

EDITOR Rebecca Glaser
DESIGNER Kathleen Petelinsek

ABOUT THE AUTHOR

Connie Colwell Miller is a writer, reader, and teacher who lives in Mankato, Minnesota. When she was little she always knew she would work with two things: kids and books. Today, her dream has come true. She has written over 80 books for kids, and she lives with four wonderful, creative children of her own.

ABOUT THE ILLUSTRATOR

Silvia Baroncelli has loved to draw since she was a child. She collaborates regularly with publishers in drawing and graphic design from her home in Prato, Italy. Her best collaborators are her four nephews, daughters Ginevra and Irene, and organized husband Tommaso. Find out more about her at silviabaroncelli.it

My name is Emmy, and I am learning to play the violin. I love to make music. When I grow up, I'm going to be a musician.

Learning the violin is difficult. I have to practice a lot and listen to my teacher. Sometimes I get tired of practicing. But then I pretend . . .

... I am Emeline Granger, first violinist and concertmaster of the Metropolitan Symphony. I have the most important role in the entire orchestra. I even have a solo!

Today's performance is starting soon. Guests are taking their seats, chatting excitedly. They can't wait to hear us perform.

The musicians are backstage. We make sure our instruments are ready. The brass and woodwind players warm up. We double-check each other's clothing.

The musicians file on stage. When the musicians are in their places, the audience applauds. After a few moments, I walk on stage and take a bow. The audience claps for me, too.

As concertmaster, I tell the musicians when to tune up. I point to the principal oboe. She plays an A. All the musicians tune their instruments to match that note. Now we're ready for the concert.

Then, the conductor appears and takes his bow. The audience applauds again. Everyone becomes completely still and silent.

The conductor lifts his baton. We lift our instruments. With a flick of the baton, the conductor tells us to begin. Like magic, the audience hears all kinds of sounds–strings, brass, reeds, and percussion.

Everything goes beautifully—even my solo! When the piece ends, the conductor's eyes are shining. He is pleased with our performance. All our practice has paid off. The audience gives us a standing ovation!

When I grow up, I'll be a great famous musician—maybe even one of the best! But right now, I know I have to practice, practice, practice!

WORDS MUSICIANS SHOULD KNOW

brass–Instruments such as trumpet, trombone, tuba, and horn.

concertmaster–Usually the first violin and he or she leads the orchestra, second only to the conductor.

percussion–Instruments played by striking, such as drums, timpani, xylophone, marimba, and piano.

principal–A musician who leads a section of instruments.

reeds–Instruments with a reed in the mouthpiece, such as oboe, clarinet, saxophone, and bassoon.

strings–Instruments played by drawing a bow across the strings or by plucking strings, such as violin, viola, cello, and string bass.

standing ovation–When an audience stands and claps at the end of a performance to show how much they liked it.

MAKE A BOX GUITAR

WHAT YOU NEED

kid-sized shoe box
paper towel tube
scissors
tape
six rubber bands
cardboard tube from a wire hanger

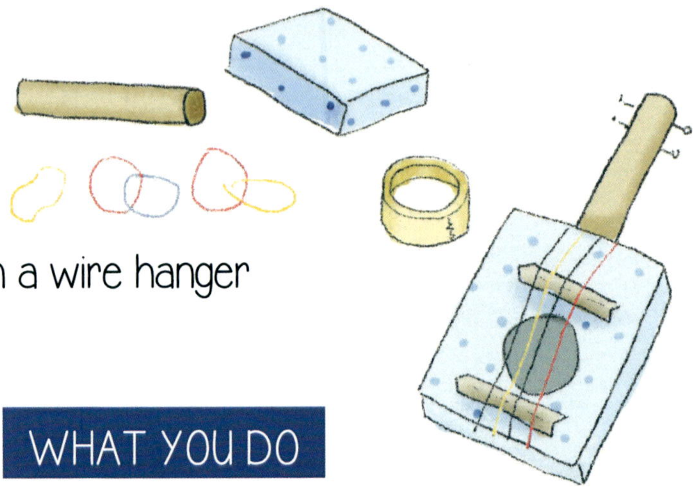

WHAT YOU DO

1. Place one end of the paper towel tube against the center of the short side of the shoe box. Trace a circle around the tube.
2. Ask an adult to help you cut out the circle.
3. Slide the tube through the hole until it hits the other end of the box. Secure with tape.
4. Cut an oval in the center of the lid, and put it back on the box.
5. Cut the tube from the hanger in half so you have two tubes. Glue the pieces above and below the oval. This will allow the "strings" to twang.
6. Stretch six rubber bands lengthwise around the box.
7. Pluck or strum the rubber bands with your fingers and try to play a tune!